Memoirs of a Mother

Edit Alaverdyan

DEDICATION

To my son Noah Hovhannisyan who chose me as his mother and helped me find my voice. My dear child thank you for trusting and believing in me.

CONTENTS

ACKNOWLEDGMENTS

My beautiful parents, thank you for the unconditional love and support. This book would not have been possible without your support. Your inner strength and courage shaped the way I process and live my life.

INTRO

When we are born, we are born with an identity and rights. An identity is who you are as a woman, you as a woman have the right to feel connected, a right for self-love and belonging. It is your human right to have an abundance. Lately, many mothers are reporting feelings of sadness and lack of connection to self. My goal is for this journal to help mothers connect back to themselves again. It is also my goal to provide a tool that can protect a mother's emotional wellbeing and instill memories that were lost. This journal is not only a memoir but also a tool you can take with you in times of mentoring or therapy sessions to help with structure. These prompts created will help and allow you to work through feelings in sessions that have not been accessed. Many women are afraid of approaching therapy due to racing thoughts. Allow Memoirs of a Mother to identify your thoughts. Before starting, allow me to provide my personal experience with the disconnection of self. I gave birth to my son in 2015 and experienced severe post-partum. During the process of working on myself, I ended up leaving my marriage of three years. During my journey, I discovered marriage, motherhood and life stressors did not provide much time for me to have for myself. Due to thinking and putting others before me, I lost complete touch with myself and dropped into the depression lane once again. I started thinking about how I can love myself and re-connect with who I am. After all, to love myself meant I can love my son and others as well. I was missing myself as a young woman, a carefree woman, strong, vibrant and grateful. I lost all of that because I made no effort for myself. I locked myself in a room for five years, feeling ashamed and disconnected. One day, a great friend drew a portrait of me, he named it "Edit behind the veil". Sparks were in the air as I looked myself in the portrait daily. The portrait was my visual board. A sense of motivation and confidence climbed my soul. From there on Momfident Women was born. I had beautiful ideas floating through my veins. Through my education and experience, I decided to push myself up from the victim chair and take charge of my life. Realistically, no one was going to do it for me. So, as your momfident creator, I present to you a journey! You are not lost or disconnect from yourself, mama. Ideally, you need support and tools to connect with that beautiful inner child again that hasn't been given much attention. I will help you and provide you with prompts. Remember to complete each page every day or night, create a time that works for you. Consistency is important mama, do not forget and do not neglect your journey. If you notice you will see each section has an age group. These prompts are geared for each age group and your previous or current developmental milestones. The process is amazing and fun. Allow yourself to enjoy this journey. Have fun mama!

0-18 MONTHS
TRUST VS. MISTRUST

Date _____

My name is.

There are two great days in your life: the day you were born and the day you find out why. William Barclay

Date _____

I was born.

Date _____

I was born in.

Date _____

I was born at. **If hospital or home, get into details which hospital.**

Date _____

When I was born, I looked like. **Skin color, hair color, eyes, weight and height**

Date _____

I slept in a.

Date _____

I had my own space to sleep and it looked like.

Date _____

I was a calm child because.

Date _____

I got my first tooth at age.

Date _____

I said my first word at age.

"A baby is God's opinion that the world should go on."

Date _____

My first words were.

Date _____

I started taking my first steps at age.

Date _____

I was taken care of or babysat by.

Date _____

I experienced illness at age. **Cancer, sickness, or disease**.

Date _____

I was ill for.

Date _____

Describe the illness process. **Ask family to help you if you are having difficulty remembering.**

Date _____

I celebrated my first birthday at.

Date _____

I had trouble trusting people growing up because.

Date _____

I had a difficult time staying with other family members because.

Date _____

I felt safe with my parents only because.

Date _____

I was attached to my parents because.

Date _____

I had play dates with.

Date _____

I could play independently by. **Please explain details**

Date _____

I was raised with both parents in the household. **If not, please explain.**

18 MONTHS -3 YEARS OF AGE AUTONOMY VS. SHAME AND DOUBT

Date _____

I started pre-school at age.

Date _____

I never went to preschool because.

Date _____

I had difficulty transitioning to preschool because.

Date _____

I cried when I was left at school because.

Date _____

I succeeded in my movement milestones by the age of. **Hopping, walking, going up the stairs, kicking a ball forward.**

Date _____

I mastered my hand and finger milestone by the age of. **Copying squares and shapes, using scissors.**

Date _____

I mastered my language milestone by the age of. **Slight storytelling, able to use words.**

Date _____

I mastered my cognitive milestones by the age of. **Naming colors, understanding a concept of names and counting, naming animals, engaging in fantasy play, making eye contact.**

Date _____

I mastered my emotional milestones by the age of. **Cooperating with other children, plays with parents, thinks about dressing self and undressing, views self, interested in new experiences, can share toys, explains in words when upset.**

Date _____

My developmental and health watch were. **These are the areas you struggled in, please list them (e.g., cannot walk, throw a ball, speak, cannot stack four blocks, ignores other children, gets upset easily, cannot use single words, lashes out, tantrums).**

3-5 YEARS OF AGE
INITIATIVE VS. GUILT

Date _____

My physical milestones in this stage were. **Where you able to dress and undress without little help?**

Date _____

I was confident and was able to write and become interested in activities because.

Date _____

I enjoyed playing with other kids and remembered a time when.

Date _____

I understood and respected feelings of others. I remember a time.

Date _____

I cooperated with friends and played nicely. I remember when.

Date _____

It was easy to comfort friends, I remember when.

Date _____

It was easy to follow directions. I remember when.

Date _____

I was obsessed with the cartoon. **Homework: to watch your childhood cartoon and write down your feelings.**

Date _____

I had no patience for.

Date _____

I remember a time being shamed.

Date _____

I was shamed for.

Date _____

My feelings when I was shamed.

Date _____

I remember feeling guilty when.

Date _____

After feeling guilty I experienced.

Date _____

I felt confident.

Date _____

I remember a time when I took control over.

Date _____

I remember being praised for being a leader.

Date _____

I remember a time I was praised for an accomplishment.

Date _____

I remember a time I was punished for.

Date _____

I remember the punishment was.

Date _____

After being punished I felt.

Date _____

I was physically and verbally abused when.

Date _____

After being abused I felt.

Date _____

I remember the abuse when. **What are your triggers**.

Date _____

I experienced trauma and what happened was.

Date _____

I remember my trauma felt like.

5-13 YEARS OF AGE
INDUSTRY VS. INFERIORITY

Date _____

I started puberty and it felt like.

Date _____

Transitioning to a young woman felt like.

Date _____

I felt like my puberty process was.

Date _____

I remember my first love.

Date _____

When I thought about my love, I had feelings of.

Date _____

I wanted to be with my first love because.

Date _____

I had _____ great in school because.

Date _____

My relations with friends and family during school was.

Date _____

I was known as the school.

Date _____

Being the school _____ I felt.

Date _____

I felt supported by my family members when.

Date _____

I remember a time I was ridiculed, and it felt.

Date _____

I wanted to be a _____ while growing up.

Date _____

I liked who I was because.

Date _____

I felt growing up was.

Date _____

I remember feelings of _____.

Date _____

I remember a time when.

Date _____

Making friends was easy for me.

Date _____

I had _____ type of a personality.

Date _____

I _____ my parents because.

Date _____

I practiced _____ religion because.

Date _____

I was very organized growing up, I remember when.

Date _____

I had a dream.

13-21 YEARS OF AGE
IDENTITY VS. CONFUSION

Date _____

I had _____ type of a personality.

Date _____

I had goals and they were.

Date _____

I had a _____ school/college process.

Date _____

My longest relationship was.

Date _____

I fell in love when.

Date _____

The strengths I possessed at this stage were.

Date _____

I felt safe being around.

Date _____

I had a _____college or educational pursuance process.

Date _____

I was ____ going to college because.

Date _____

My travel experience was ____. I remember when.

Date _____

I remember being confused about who I was because.

Date _____

I remember reaching out for help from.

Date _____

I remember a time I had to defend myself because.

Date _____

I remember accomplishing.

Date _____

I remember a time I learned ____ and it felt.

Date _____

My accomplishments felt like.

21-39 YEARS OF AGE
INTIMACY VS. ISOLATION

Date _____

Love means.

Date _____

Love feels like.

Date _____

I fell in love when.

Date _____

I feel that love needs.

Date _____

For me to love someone, they need to have. **List the qualities you are looking for.**

Date _____

I experienced loneliness when.

Date _____

I remember feeling lonely.

Date _____

I feel commitment is about.

Date _____

To love myself I need to.

Date _____

I love myself because.

Date _____

List at least ten qualities you bring into your relationship with friend and family.

Date _____

List ten qualities you bring into your love life.

Date _____

List five areas you would like to change about your relationship.

Date _____

List five boundaries you can utilize to protect yourself from being hurt.

Date _____

I would like to possess ten healthy boundaries and they are.

Mothers Journey

"I never knew how strong I was until I was placed on a delivery bed"

Edit Alaverdyan

In this section of the journal, we are going to be diving into your birthing process, whether you have adopted or birthed. This process is going to get you more in touch with your emotions and feelings while you were pregnant. Mothers of the world, I have been working with mothers struggling or recovering from Post-Partum Depression for about two years. Many women including I were reporting loss of connection to self. Now birthing a child for many has allowed the discovery of self, however, the timing and transitioning has not given room for self-care. Becoming a mother is an amazing gift, however, it can become overwhelming if things are not managed correctly. Writing from personal experience, becoming a mother changed me into a stronger and wiser person with a different mindset. I became a wonder woman with no time to save the world. The timing was a big issue. No time to shower, no time for hair and nails, no time to clean, self-care to read to write. Treating mothers with PPD I leaned that timing was one of the major reasons for disconnecting from self. There was not enough time in the day to take a moment to breathe and remember something fun, interesting or something from the past. There is another portion to this, some women experience traumatic birth. I have also created some journal prompts to give you the safe space and time to journal about your feelings and full experience of birth, this is a great way to keep track so that when you decide to get mentoring you can take your journal during your sessions as guidance and notes. Let's get started, Mama.

Date _____

My journey to become pregnant was.

Date _____

I felt ____ when I found out I was pregnant.

Date _____

I felt like pregnancy was going to be.

Date _____

I disclosed the news to my partner by.

Date _____

Describe the reaction of you and your partner about the pregnancy.

Date _____

My first trimester was. **Describe physical experience.**

Date _____

My first trimester was. **Describe emotional experiences**.

Date _____

Describe your first trimester. **Describe emotional experiences continuation**

Date _____

Describe the people who have supported you during your first trimester.

Date _____

My second trimester was. **Physical experiences**

Date _____

My second trimester was. **Emotional experience**

Date _____

My second trimester was. **Emotional experience continuation**

Date _____

Shopping for my baby felt like.

Date _____

When I was decorating my childs room I felt.

Date _____

My support system is.

Date _____

My third trimester was. **Physical experience**

Date _____

Describe about your discomforts.

Date _____

My third trimester was. **Emotional experience**

Date _____

My third trimester was. **Emotional experience continuation**

Date _____

I chose to deliver my baby at.

Date _____

My delivery process was.

Date _____

My delivery Process was. **Continuation**

Date _____

I was in labor for _____ because.

Birthing a child allowed me to find my voice.

Edit Alaverdyan

The delivery process can be traumatic for some mothers. In this next section lets write about your delivery process.

Remember trauma does not mean the event, trauma means the response your nervous system had after the event. So, if you had nightmares, flashback, bad dreams PPD, those are a response system after a traumatic event.

Date _____

I experienced a traumatic delivery process because.

Date _____

After delivery I experienced.

Date _____

I felt.

Date _____

I had ____ help me.

Date _____

I had a _____ support system and it felt like.

Date _____

I was afraid because.

Date _____

I was worried because.

Date _____

I felt depression for.

Date _____

I cried because.

Date _____

I was disconnected from my child because I felt.

Date _____

I had understanding from.

Date _____

I needed more help with.

Date _____

When I asked for help, I felt.

Date _____

I helped myself by.

Date _____

I have these people who continually helped me.

Date _____

The strengths I possess are.

Date _____

During birth I learned that I am.

Date _____

I would like to improve_____ about myself.

Date _____

List all boundaries you possess firmly.

Date _____

I practice assertiveness by.

Date _____

My number one influencer is.

Date _____

Boundaries are.

Date _____

I love my boundaries they protect me when.

Date _____

I experience negative thoughts when I think about.

Date _____

I feel _____ when I have negative thoughts.

I have provided journal prompts for you to dig dip and allow yourself to think about things that need attention. I want you to use the prompts and your answers as a way of appreciation of yourself. Let it be known beautiful, I'm very proud of you for continuing to the journal, you have invested time and effort connecting with yourself. You should already have a sense of your experience and sense of connection to yourself again. Remembering things in the past can help you re-connect and find the answers you were looking for.

In this last section, you are going to journal about present moments. This section is geared more towards gratitude, goals, wants, and self-awareness. Notice throughout the entire journal I have prompted you with "I" or "I feel". I allow you to connect with yourself using mostly I statements. You Rock beautiful Mom keep going. This next section will make you smile.

Date _____

I am thankful for.

Date _____

I'm grateful for.

Date _____

What helped you become thankful and appreciate what you have.

Date _____

What helped you become grateful and appreciate what you have

Date _____

Today I feel.

Date _____

Creating a safe place for your self is very important beautiful mama. It could be anywhere in the house. (e.g., a desk with flowers a chair so you can think unwind and recharge) If you do not have a space to recharge. Think about creating one. Your own private Sanctuary.

I have a safe space to recharge, and it looks like.

Date _____

A good thing that happened today is.

Date _____

Write about something nice you saw another person do, and how it made you feel.

Date _____

Today I was relaxed when.

Date _____

Today I had fun when.

Date _____

Today I felt grateful when.

Date _____

Today I felt thankful when.

Date _____

Today I accomplished.

Date _____

Today I laughed when.

Date _____

Today I felt happy when.

Date _____

Organization is important busy mama. Get a planner and start organizing everything you need to accomplish? (e.g., laundry, dishes, reading, cooking, nails) whatever the case might be start planning and creating a to do list. It will decrease your anxiety tremendously.

Today I felt organized when.

Date _____

I enjoy _____ company because they make me feel.

Date _____

I'm excited for the future because.

Date _____

The life lessons I have learned are.

Date _____

I admire.

Date _____

I can always trust.

Date _____

I'm proud of myself for.

Date _____

An experience I'm lucky to have had.

Date _____

Something beautiful I saw.

Date _____

A motivation I had today.

Date _____

My goals for 2020.

Date _____

My boundaries for 2020.

Date _____

I love the smell of.

Date _____

I'm thankful and grateful when my partner.

Date _____

I'm grateful and thankful when my kids.

Date _____

I'm grateful and thankful when my support system.

Date _____

My values are.

Date _____

My strong beliefs are.

Date _____

I love myself when.

Date _____

I apologize to myself for.

Date _____

I respect myself for.

Date _____

I promise myself to.

Date _____

I will take care of myself by.

Date _____

I will never neglect or disrespect myself because.

Date _____

I will approach myself gently and respectfully when making a mistake because.

Date _____

I promise myself to always.

Date _____

I promise to motivate myself by.

Date _____

I promise to speak to myself kindly by using words.

Date _____

I promise to never compare myself to anyone and instead to.

Date _____

I offer the world.

Date _____

I promise myself to follow people who motivate me on Social Media.

Date _____

I offer my family.

Date _____

I'm amazing and powerful because.

Date _____

I promise to never hurt myself again by.

Date _____

I am the best mother to my children because.

Date _____

My self-care days are going to be.

Congratulations mama you have finished your journey to self-connection. Enjoy your Momfidence and remember to be grateful and thankful.

Go rock the world

Repeat out loud daily for optimal results.

- ❖ I love myself
- ❖ I deserve love
- ❖ I deserve respect
- ❖ I deserve compassion
- ❖ I deserve abundance
- ❖ I will have everything I desire
- ❖ I will have health money love and belonging
- ❖ I am enough
- ❖ I am happy
- ❖ I am beautiful
- ❖ I am Intelligent
- ❖ I am great mother
- ❖ I am strong
- ❖ I am momfident
- ❖ I am loved
- ❖ I am sexy
- ❖ I am Powerful
- ❖ I have power
- ❖ I will remember to approach myself as I approach an innocent child in times of a mistake.

ABOUT THE AUTHOR

Edit Alaverdyan was born and raised in Hrazdan Armenia, she migrated to the United States of America at age nine, from then on, she had a passion for humanitarianism and Psychology. Edit graduated from the University of Phoenix, earning her bachelor's degree in psychology and a master's degree in Marriage and Family Child Therapy. Edit conducted two years of her training at BHC Alhambra Hospital working with Acute patients in mental health distress followed by extensive experience with eating disorder patients. While working at Reasons Eating Disorder Recovery Center, she gained extensive experience conducting various groups and Psychotherapy approaches. Edit has been invited to several schools such as Cal State University Northridge specifically for her Psycho-educational courses and Panel speeches on individuals struggling with Grief and Loss as well as Depression. Edit has been known for her psycho-educational courses on various research-based practices. Edit is continuing her education with a Doctorate in Health Administration. She has been helping various mental health organizations consulting and implementing various programs by adding the approach to advanced study and research in the applied science and practice of professional management. She is also a Mindset Mentor for mothers and women struggling with connection to self.

Made in the USA
Lexington, KY
08 November 2019